listen
before you go

akhira

MW00958688

listen before you go

Copyright © 2024 by akhira

independently published

ISBN: 9798883177483

All rights reserved.

instagram.com/dyingful
instagram.com/akhirapoetry
twitter.com/akhirapoetry
tiktok.com/@akhirapoetry

listen before you go

Tue, 6 Feb at 09.13

 01:07

 01:34

▶ ⅢⅢⅢⅢⅢⅢⅢⅢⅢⅢⅢⅢ 0:11

please listen, when you listen to this, don't reply to it, okay. i don't want you to reply to it. i have heard what you had to say, now you just listen to what i say and then just leave it as it is. take care, and thank you so much for everything, goodbye akhira.

Seen just now

 1:00

akhira listen, you didn't pick up which is fine i guess, it's for the better. please stop texting me after this. i can't not with you blocking me and then you coming back. and the constant making accounts to message me. that's not.. enough, enough is enough. you didn't hear me out, and you just blocked me. and then you just expect me to be "oh it's fine." it's not fine. i can't do this anymore, this is it, this is the last time we are talking. thank you for being there for me, and for helping me with everything. and it's not about me waiting 4 months for you, i would have waited for you longer but the way you just left, you didn't give me a reason... you didn't let me explain to you what things actually were and what was going on and you just left like that and you blocked me, that was extremely disrespectful. and i get that, after what i told you, of course i didn't expect you to be happy about it, i knew you were upset about what i told you but i didn't know how upset.

Seen just now

3

 1:00

i have no hard feelings towards you, and i hope you feel the same way. and i wanna just give the both of us, a very calm ending, i don't want things to be dramatic, i don't want things to be blown out of proportion. i think it's best that the both of us just like completely move on from this, and never look back. because this will never stop. so i wish you the best, and i hope everything works out for you. but i can't, i can not anymore, instead of talking to me, and resolving things with me, and you just blocked me, and i told myself if he blocks me after this, i will never look back, and that's exactly what i did. and i'm not looking back right now either. i hope everything works out for you and thank you so much for being there for me and helping me through everything and giving me so much advice, you have done a lot, so thank you so much for that.

and because that i respect you so much, that i feel like it's incorrect of me to move on from this whole situation, with anything other than, good feelings, i don't want there to be any ill intentions or ill feelings between the both of us, i hope you understand that.

and i can't find closure
in the last voice message
you left a week ago
so i cry and call you again
even with no dial tone
till your friends tell me
to leave you alone

listen before you go

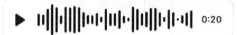 0:20

you can keep me blocked

act like i don't exist

lie on my name

blame me for eyerything that happened,

but you won't forget that i was the only
one who listened to you and knew the
real you

you won't forget how many times
i chose to stay when i should've left.

you won't forget the times i helped you
get through the situation nobody knew
about, even when i was struggling
myself

Seen just now

▶ ·❙❙❙❙❙❙·❙❙❙❙·❙·❙❙❙❙❙··❙❙❙·❙❙·❙❙·· 0:17

i deleted your pictures
your texts
your number
but i couldn't delete
your face
your voice
and our memories

▶ ⅰⅼⅰⅰⅰⅼⅼⅼⅰⅼⅰⅰⅰⅼⅰⅰⅼⅼⅼⅰⅰⅰⅰ‧ⅰⅰ‧ 0:28

why is this so hard??

Because you're used to waking up with the feeling of knowing he's yours and you're used to going to sleep knowing that you're gonna have him to wake up to. It's all about what you're used to. You're used to having him. your mind is used to talking to him everyday. It's just like a bad habit, it's hard to quit. But once you do, you'll realize how bad it was for you and how much better you deserve. It's all in your head.

Seen just now

0:08

can we start over?
can we be strangers again?
let me introduce myself
we can laugh and talk
and relearn what we already know
and come up with new inside jokes
and create new memories
and give each other a second chance.

▶ ᵗᵗˡˡ·ˡ|·ˡˡˡˡ···ˡˡ···ˡ|ˡˡˡ||ˡˡ 0:22

I want to text you all the time and see how you're doing, but I know I can't because deep down I know it won't change anything. It sucks because I thought things were going so well, but then one day came and everything changed and now I'm up at 2 am wondering how and why everything went wrong and what I did. Why I wasn't good enough for you. I find myself looking at old texts and pictures and I remember how happy I was and how happy we were. And all I can do is question how I ended up here, without you.

Seen just now

you're not in my life anymore,
but i still feel like,
i'd be cheating on you
if i go out with someone else

listen before you go

how i wish i had more time to get to know you..

how i wish you gave me a chance to love you

how i wish you didn't end what haven't even started yet

i will always wonder what our life could've been if you took the risk with me

Seen just now

▶ ‖‖·‖‖‖‖·‖‖‖‖‖‖·‖‖‖‖··‖‖‖··‖‖‖‖ 0:23

i never stopped waiting for you
when my phone lights up,
there's still a sinking feeling
when it's not you who texted me.
i'm still waiting.
i'll always be waiting.
but you won't come back.
and i know it, but
i rather wait for the impossibility
with you, than settle
for the possibility
of anyone else

▶ ᴵᴵᴵᵘᴵᴵᴵᴵᴵᴵᴵᴵᴵᴵᴵᴵᴵᴵᴵᴵᴵᴵᴵᴵᴵᴵᴵᴵᴵᴵᴵᴵᴵᴵᴵᴵᴵᴵᴵ 0:11

i miss your smile. miss your voice, i miss the way you talk to me, i miss the way you made me feel so happy, i miss the way you looked at me, i miss your notifications, i miss our conversation, i miss when you were mine, i miss our memories, i miss our sweet texts and words, i miss us and it hurts me whenever i miss you.

Seen just now

 0:10

i never liked that song
but once i knew it is your favorite,
i listened to it on repeat
and it became one of the best
songs i've ever heard

— *the night we met*

 0:37

Hey. I know we haven't spoken in a while, and I'm really sorry about that. I just kept telling myself that if you still wanted to be with me, you would call me, but I couldn't take it any longer. So here it is.

I miss you so much, way more than I should. Every time I see your face and those brown eyes of yours my heart breaks a little more. You're always on my mind, and I keep wondering if I ever cross yours. Please talk to me. You told me actions speak thousand words? And I'm telling you silence speaks a million more. I don't know if you still care about me, or even if you ever did in the first place. Please just say something.

Seen just now

our goodbye
were divided into two
one for the love
one for the friendship

— you were my best friend too

listen before you go

0:28

you said you love me

but you ignore me

you dry text me and escape me

you leave me alone

you make me feel like you don't want to
talk to me anymore

you make me feel like i'm annoying

you make me feel like i'm not important
to you

you make me feel so confused and
overthink about our relationship

you asked me to stop overthinking but
you are the one who made me overthink

Seen just now

everything that we had,
everything that you said,
was it all just lies?

 0:11

i know that i'm still waiting for you..

and i know that shouldn't be..

but i can't let go of you.

i hate that so much..

but i'm always gonna wait for you..

even if you're never coming back..

cause i love you too much to let go..

i don't wanna forget about the memories that we made..

i love you forever and always...

Seen just now

i hate that i can't hate you

0:06

I tried to hate you. I really tried. But how could i hate the person who made me love myself. The one person who lit up my entire world with just his smile. Made me feel things i never thought were possible to feel...

Seen just now

 0:20

i wish i had hugged you when i had
the chance because now it's 2 am and
you're gone and all i want is your touch

0:11

you know what, you can leave. okay? go ahead. but don't forget to take the times where we would talk for hours about life, and the times where i would call you when i had good news, and the times where i would cry to you on bad days, and the times where you would walk me out to my car, and the times where you met my family, and the times where i would text you at 3 am, and the times where i would simply look into your deep brown eyes and genuinely smile. LEAVE. DO IT. but don't you DARE say this was nothing. and especially, don't you DARE leave this all behind. i was there. i saw the way you looked at me.

Seen just now

▶ |||||||||||||||||||||||||||||||||||||| 0:11

it's so sad, that even now,
even after everything, it's still you.
i still want it to be you

you can't love someone unless you love
yourself first

bullshit

i have never loved myself

but you?

oh god

i loved you so much i forgot what hating
myself felt like.

Seen just now

▶ ıl|||·ı|ııııı·|||ıı·ı|ı|·|·|ıı 0:33

i remember the first time
we started talking.
you were the reason
i got my laugh back.
the reason i fell asleep
with a smile on my face.
the reason i had motivation
to do things again.
the reason why my problems
didn't seem so bad.
you truly have made my life
better by just being in it

my "iloveyou" without saying it.

i put your birthday as my phone password

i pin your chat

i still keep your picture

making a playlist with all the songs you showed

setting an alarm for the time you usually wake up, so i can text you "good morning"

adding your city to my weather app

saving screenshots of the duration of our facetime calls

your name is in my autocorrect

Seen just now

 0:21

i still care about you,
we have not talked
to each other in a while,
but that doesn't mean
if you called me tonight,
that i wouldn't pick up

 0:09

are you still waiting for her?

yeah, why?

aren't you tired of waiting?

well, i feel tired of waiting sometimes but... i really want this girl back and she's the only girl i want. i made a promise to her that i wont find or love someone else again if she's not the one i will love. that's why im still watching her to comeback, i miss her every single day.

Seen just now

i have been staying awake at nights,
wondering if i should call you

listen before you go

 0:07

worst feeling???

when you miss someone but can't tell them because the situation is not the same anymore.

Seen just now

 0:14

we lost each other by waiting
for the other to call first

0:11

I miss you...

You don't miss me. You miss the attention. You miss the second chances. You miss the power. Sadly for you, I don't miss it and I don't want it back. You can't tell me that you miss me. Not after everything you did to push me away.

Seen just now

 0:10

i miss you
i miss us
i miss having you
to talk to
whenever i wanted
but i know
i have to move on,
because this is pointless

I miss you so much. One bad chapter does not mean our story is over. True love has a habit of coming back. I'm sorry about what happened between us.

Don't write paragraphs about how much you loved me because, when was alone my darkest hours, you weren't the one Who stood besides me to make sure I was alright. You were special to me. You were the only one who i wouldn't mind losing sleep for, the only one who I can never get tired of talking to, and the only one who crosses my mind constantly throughout the day. You were the only one who can make me smile without trying, bring down my mood without the intention to and affect my emotions with every action of yours. I can't explain with just words how much you meant to me, you were the only one I was afraid of losing and the one I wanted to keep in my life. But now, when they ask you about me and you find yourself thinking back on all of our memories, I hope you ache in regret as truth hits you like a bullet and you find yourself replying: "she loved me more than anyone else the entire world and I destroyed her."

 0:13

i miss you from time to time
but i'll cut off my hand
before i ever text you again

 0:17

Do you miss him?

No, actually I don't. I miss the person I fell in love with, but not the person they are right now. That boy you see is not the person that I knew, he's an entirely different person now. I don't know what made him change, I held on for months, hoping that he would still be there. But there's only so much a person can hold onto before giving up, and I'm quite sure he isn't going to come back anyway. I tried giving him my best and it wasn't enough and that's fine. I've moved on from him and I'm happy now, but I will forever be in love with the person he used to be.

Seen just now

it hurts to wait for someone
who's never coming back again

 0:33

Why don't you answer me? I'm getting nervous about you..

Okay, I'm trying not to text you, I really am.. but I think that's too hard for me, cause you've been a part of my everyday routine. I really love when we're talking for hours at nights. And when we're not texting each other, then I just feel empty and just literally sad. I want you, just you as you are. I want you and me to be an "us", even on our worst days. Because since I've met you my life has been better.

I need time...

truth is i didn't expect to
get this attached to you

▶ ||||||||||||||||||||||••••••••••|| 0:35

Hey, I just wanted to make sure you are okay..

I know you are upset with me but I just wanted you to know that I care...

you really think i'm okay?? after everything that you put me through you except me to be okay? and don't pretend like you care, if you really cared you wouldn't have lied to me and you wouldn't have made me believe that i actually meant something to you. What you did hurt. and no i am not okay. you don't understand how much i cared about you. you lost someone who truly would've given up the world for you.

Seen just now

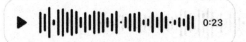 0:23

i miss how close we were

 0:16

Just text me if you need me if you have
a problem...

I need you have a problem, my problem
is that i need you. And Thate that I do
But I don't think you need me as much
as I need you, You don't seem to care
anymore about me. But, I still care
about you and, always will no matter
what. I want to move on from you so
bad but, something is making me stay
with you. Maybe it's that if I stay around
maybe one day you'll come around and
want me back. I don't want to wait
around for something that may or may
not happen. I don't want to miss out on
my life just on one person. And I
shouldn't have depended all my
happiness on you. But now that you've
stopped caring, it's my turn to stop
trying for you.

Seen just now

you knew what you were doing
and you knew it would hurt me,
but somehow that didn't stop you

 0:22

Maybe we should just break up?

I AM SO SICK OF THIS!! Every time I'm the one that has to stop this relationship from falling apart, You can't handle one argument without mentioning us breaking up. I'm sick of keeping us together and being the only one putting effort into us. It's so easy for you to just resort to ending it, taking the easy way out. I can not be the glue to our relationship anymore. Even if I have to do the HARD thing for myself and leave, I will. if it means being happy for once, I'll go. Maybe I won't be happy straight away, but I'll work on myself. I'm sick of trying to make you happy when you can't even fight for me, when you can't even try getting through the rough patches... When you can't try for us. I love you, but I'm losing myself in you while you're finding yourself in places that I'm not apart of.

Seen just now

i wanted to say

"don't leave me,"

but i didn't,
not this time
because i'm so tired of
begging you to love me

0:16

So I'm here to say that you mean everything to me and that I love you no matter what.

k

Seen just now

▶ ▎▎▍▎▍▎▏▎▎▍▎▎▍▍▎▎▍▍▏▏▎▎▍▎▍▍▏▏▏▎▍▏▍▎ 0:11

i wish she
loved
me
like i loved her

▶ |ıı||ı|ııı|·|·|||ı|||ıııı||·ıııı· 0:13

you are stupid for falling in love with her

how?

because you aren't going to be loved back

First of all I'm not stupid for falling in love with her no matter he loves me back or not. Don't you dare say my love for someone is stupid, because when I love someone you know It means something you know it's special I love her because she makes me happy even when I'm not it's because when I look at her I see my future because when I'm with her, I feel something that I've never felt. She can love someone else but that won't stop me from loving her. So go ahead and call me stupid but just know that you're stupid for thinking that you can only love someone who chooses to love you back.

Seen just now

▶ ·⑴⑾⑾⑾·⑾·⑾⑾⑾·⑾·⑾··⑾·⑾·· 0:17

it's a brave thing
to love someone
who doesn't love you,
but at some point
you need to realize
that you're worth
being loved back

listen before you go

 0:11

what's wrong?

i'm still in love with you.

Seen just now

one day you are
going to miss
my boring texts,
my random calls,
my silly questions,
you'll miss my fight,
my mood swings,
my arguments,
my possessives
and my insecurities.
but most of all
you'll miss the way
i cared for you

Did you ever love me?

Because you gave up on me.
Remember?

Are you being serious right now?

You know I did. loved you with all I had
but that still wasn't good enough for
you. You left. Many times. But stayed I
always stayed. But you can't expect me
to stay when all you did was push me
away. I haven't done anything but love
you, but you were the one who was
watching it all fall apart. I was the only
thing keeping this relationship together.
Don't come here and blame this on me,
because I can't believe what I did for us.

So I think the real question is did you
ever love me?

Seen just now

0:20

she hurt me more than anyone ever has,
but she loved me better than anyone
ever did, too.

listen before you go

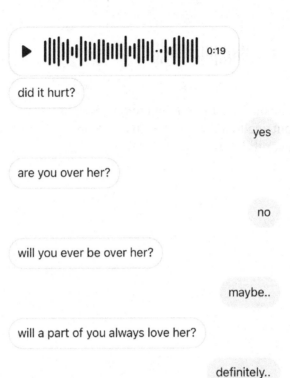

did it hurt?

yes

are you over her?

no

will you ever be over her?

maybe..

will a part of you always love her?

definitely..

Seen just now

a part of me is moving on, but
another part is still stuck with you

 0:19

I don't wanna lose you..

And I don't want to wait around hoping that someday you decide that I am what you want

Seen just now

▶ |||||||||||||||||||||||||||||||||| 0:11

i'd be lying if i told you,
that losing you was
something i could handle

 0:20

Do you want him back?

You know I do. But like I can't. Yet at least. Like if he wants that, and asks, I have to tell him no. I mean obviously I want to, but I can't let him think that I'm some item he can just take off a shelf and use when he wants and then when he's done using me, he'll just put me right back. I respect myself more that than that.

Seen just now

 0:20

you didn't love me,
because you don't
destroy the person
that you love

 0:22

I never meant for this to happen

I'm sure you didn't. But you know what though? **** you and *** your no-good bs intentions. If you were clear enough, if you made the effort to show you loved me, maybe, Just maybe it wouldn't have happened like this. Maybe it wouldn't have happened at all. But here we are, me sobbing over you and your fake apologies becaue you don't care and I care too much. I gave a good bit of me to you and you took it for granted, all of it. This is where we say goodbye because I'm done being used and mistreated and wronged. I'm worth more than you and your dumb mind games. Have a GREAT rest of your life and don't even BOTHER coming up at 4am with those texts because "you're sorry".

Seen just now

▶ ᶦᶦᶦᶦ·ᶦᶦᶦᶦᶦᶦᶦᶦ·ᶦᶦᶦᶦᶦᶦᶦᶦᶦᶦᶦᶦ·ᶦᶦᶦᶦ 0:33

there we go again
with your mixed signals
and my overthinking

listen before you go

How do you know when it's over?

I guess when you feel the need to ask.

Seen just now

▶ ||||·||||||·|·||····|||||····||||·|| 0:11

do right people with wrong timing
ever realize it?

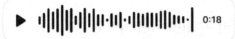 0:18

I love you

don't you dare do this again, I loved you, but you never loved me. you never did I was just your cigarette that you would light up when you were bored, and put out when you were done, I loved you, but you left me, for someone better. and now you're trying to light me up again. but I've gotten over you. I truly did love you, I loved you so much, but I guess you never wanted to feel the same way.

Seen just now

i've prayed for you on nights
i didn't pray for myself

i don't tell you this enough but, i'm so thankful for you. thank you for coming into my life. for making me smile. for making me laugh. for making me happy. i'm thankful that god sent you and i'm thankful that you found me.

Seen just now

and even if we never
talk again please
remember that i am
forever changed
by who you are
and what you
meant to me

I really hope I'm enough for you. Sometimes I feel like I'm not, and that scares me because I think you'll find someone who is. Someone who can give you everything I can't. Someone "better" than me. Is it crazy of me to feel this way? Please tell me it is. Tell me I'm more than enough. Tell me you'll always be here.

Seen just now

she saw you.
she met you.
she wanted you.
she liked you.
she chased you.
she got you.
she had you.
she got bored.
and she left you

listen before you go

 0:09

you love her, don't you?

she's not mine to love..

but you still do?

more than he ever will..

Seen just now

i loved you
even on bad days
when you felt
unlovable

listen before you go

i just miss her so much

she don't care about you

i miss you so much i cry myself to sleep

 0:23

i broke my own damn heart by continuously creating fantasies in my head of us being together, pretending that you would someday love me again. but deep down within, i knew you would never love me the way i wanted you to.

Seen just now

 0:22

no, the problem
wasn't our love
the problem was that
i wanted it too much,
wanted you too much
and you didn't want it enough

Why did you stop trying if you knew you loved her?

Because strong people will automatically stop trying if they feel unwanted. They won't fix it or beg. They will just walk away.

Seen just now

i feel so stupid when i text her
and she never reply back

listen before you go

Wait why'd you stop talking to me?

I felt like I was bothering you..

Seen just now

so if i don't text first, we will not talk?

listen before you go

 0:17

all i want is nothing more...

than to get that "i miss you, can we try again" text.

Seen just now

▶ |||ıı||||||ıı|ı·||··ıı||··|ııı||| 0:11

i missed you today and thought
about all the things you used to say

 0:07

when those texts start getting shorter with you they're getting longer with someone else..

Seen just now

it starts with late replies...

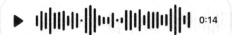
0:14

last night, I hung out with some friends and cheated on you...

Don't worry, I did something worse...

what?

Stayed home and trusted you..

Seen just now

 0:14

the worst pain is getting hurt by
a person you explained your pain to

 0:14

i'm sorry.

you're sorry? really? because if you were sorry, you wouldn't have left me crying on my bedroom floor, with a broken heart, and messed up makeup. you wouldn't have had to even witness that, because if you were really sorry, you wouldn't have hurt me. but guess what? you did. and you don't get to say sorry, so you can feel better about yourself. no. you don't get to do that. you left me there, to pick myself up. and i couldn't. and then, when someone else came along, and picked up my broken pieces, and hugged my broken pieces back together, you're sorry? no you don't get to be free of the guilt.

Seen just now

88

i wish i could go back to the day i met you and just walk away because honestly, it would've saved me so much hurt and pain.

 0:18

why are you so mean?

because the best way not to get your
heart broken is to pretend you don't
have one.

Seen just now

loving someone doesn't always mean you fight
for them, sometimes loving someone means
letting them go.

fine i guess this is where we end things

Whatever. I'm not fighting for you to stay in my life anymore, people leave me all the time, I'm not gonna change who I am for somebody else. I'm not going to be somebody I'm not because people don't like who I am. If you're into me, you're into me for who I am now, not for who you want me to be. You wanna leave? Leave. It's not going to effect me. Just another one I'll add to the list.

Seen just now

i let you in and you completely destroyed me

▶ |||||||·|·|||||||||||||·|·||||||||·· 0:23

I was the one...

Let me refresh your memory a bit. I was
the one who listened to your probems. I
was the one who actually cared about
you. I was the one who stuck around
even when everyone told me to leave. I
was the one who stood up for you. I was
the one who loved you even when you
gave me every reason not to. Lastly,
I was the one who was there for you
when no one else was.

Seen just now

you destroyed me and i apologized

listen before you go

I miss you.

No wait

I miss the old you that actually cared about me.

Seen just now

the saddest part in life is saying goodbye to
someone you wish to spend your lifetime with

▶ ||||||||||••••|•||••••|••||||•||•|||• 0:21

I think the worst thing you could do to someone emotionally is just stop speaking to them without an explanation. like do you have any idea what that does to their self esteem?? they will sit for hours at a time & just think of every single bad thing about themselves & wonder if that's why but still not know. it tears them apart, makes them notice every little flaw about them, makes them hate themselves but even more crushes any bit of trust they had in their body. i don't care that you don't want to speak to me anymore but tell me why, don't leave me in the dark about it.

Seen just now

i just wanted a kinder goodbye

 0:10

i wanted to let you know that im proud of you

you're dealing with a lot whether you like to admit it or not and you make it through everyday

you woke up today, and you're okay and for that i am grateful

Seen just now

we won't forget each other, right?

 0:13

I know you moved on and don't want me in your life. I know i'm the last person you want to talk to but I know you're going through it and feel alone. I'm sorry i fucked up and i'm sorry i played a part in hurting you. I know everything you've been through and I still managed to idk. I feel like the worst person in the world. It hurts me to see you like this. You deserve the world and i'm sorry i couldn't give it to you. You gave it to me idk why i didn't see it then.

having to lose me just to appreciate me is insane. please leave me alone for good and i hope you heal lol

Seen just now

 0:20

you realize how much
you truly miss someone
when something happens,
good or bad, and the only
person you want to tell is
the one person who isn't there.

 0:08

Trust me I love you so much!

Why don't you take my love seriously?

Last time I took somebody too serious,
I didn't smile for 7 months.

Seen just now

it hurts when the person you can't forget,
forgets you.

Why are you single?

Because my idea of love is too real for this fake world.

Seen just now

maybe we will never talk again but at
least i got to be liked by you at one point,
and it was the best feeling ever

listen before you go

with all the smiles you brought me, i never thought that you could cause me so many tears.

Seen just now

we bonded over poetry and chocolate cake
you told me your favorite book
and i read it the next day

— *something wonderful*

 0:20

she felt like home, i know i'll miss her forever.

Seen just now

please tell me
how i am supposed
to move on when
the absence of you
is everywhere i look?

— *you were my everything*

listen before you go

▶ |ıııı·ıl|ıı|ııı|ıı|·ı|ı|ıııı·ıı| 0:11

i think i'd miss you even if we never met

Seen just now

i'm caught between wanting this to be
over and wishing we could go back

0:17

i let you love me,
i let you take care of me,
i let you do things to me,
no one was allowed to do before.

Seen just now

we were, then we weren't

listen before you go

hopefully one day you'll realize
how much i really care for you

Seen just now

just because i learned how to live without
you doesn't mean i ever really wanted to

listen before you go

▶ ı··ıⱼ··ıｨ||||||ｨ··ｨ|ıｨ|ı|ı|ｨ|ıｨ 0:12

i'm worried that nothing else will
ever feel enough again after you

Seen just now

i think that maybe i would
always let you come back

listen before you go

i need you to be happy,
i need one of us to be happy.

Seen just now

"even at my worst?"

even at your worst.

listen before you go

why do you think we met?

Seen just now

i don't know what we are,
but i miss what we were

 0:14

you can't force them
to love you or want you,
but one day you'll make
them realize what they lost.

Seen just now

you will lose yourself
trying to hold on to
someone who doesn't
care about losing you

listen before you go

0:09

you are the reason
i trust my trust issues again

Seen just now

▶ |||ıı||||ıı|ı|ı··ıı||···|ııı||| 0:11

you will never know just how much
i would give up to have you back
in my life..

listen before you go

i should be sleeping, but
i'm still awake thinking of you.

Seen just now

i fall in love with people
who don't love me back
and i tell myself that my
love for them is so real
that even when they don't
love me, i still love them
...

because heartbreak
has taught me love
in the wrong way

— *unrequited love*

listen before you go

▶ ᴨᴨ‖‖ᴨᴨᴨᴨᴨᴨᴨᴨᴨ‖‖ᴨᴨ‖ 0:05

and just like that i lost you...

Seen just now

and i would let go of everything
just to hold your hand again

listen before you go

▶ ··|··||··||··|||·|···||··· |||| 0:03

we never made it, did we?

Seen just now

it's driving me insane how i can't have you

you broke my heart in every way a
person can break someone else's heart
and yet here i am still thinking of you

Seen just now

we're only haunted by people,
we refuse to let go

.

 0:13

look, i don't hate you,
i don't even not like you
i'm just done.
done with the hurt,
done with the waiting,
done with the wanting,
the needing.
no, i don't hate you,
i'm just done with you.

Seen just now

i miss her
and she misses me
but we both think
we are better off
without each other
but perhaps that's
just a big lie
we are both
hiding behind

listen before you go

0:06

you pushed me away
when all i wanted
was to be next to you
that's what broke my heart

Seen just now

 0:09

there is a spot in my heart that will
never belong to anyone else but you

listen before you go

you only missed my voice
when nobody else called you

Seen just now

it is what it is

*"i pray every night that we get
back together in the future"*

listen before you go

i broke all my rules just to be with you

Seen just now

i spent months moving on
and one text from you
brought me back to
square one

listen before you go

just because i can't have you doesn't mean i will stop praying for you

Seen just now

she was so broken from her past that
even after he showered her with love,
she bathed him with her pain.

listen before you go

why did you leave me,
when i needed you the most?
why did you leave me,
at my lowest?

Seen just now

i miss you but i know
you are not good for me

listen before you go

i was addicted to the way
you pretended...

Seen just now

you know you love someone
when pain is never a reason to leave

listen before you go

you didn't even tell me why, you just decided i wasn't good enough for you anymore and left, and that's how it ended.

Seen just now

 0:13

deep down, you know exactly where you
stand with someone, hope blurs the lines
a bit but, you know.

listen before you go

0:21

are you up?

always

can you sleep on the phone with me
please

of course

Seen just now

can we go back and
try again please?

listen before you go

 0:10

busy?

free for you

busy for others

stop being so cute

cute for you

rude for others

Seen just now

it hurts when you know you can never
be with someone but you still can't
stop yourself falling for them

listen before you go

i'm still waiting for your message

Seen just now

▶ ᐧ||||ᐧ|||ᐧ|ᐧ|||ᐧ|ᐧ|ᐧ||ᐧᐧ||ᐧ|ᐧᐧ 0:17

you were my favorite unkept promise.
my favorite what if.
my favorite almost.
my favorite *"maybe in a different lifetime."*
my favorite unfinished story.

0:04

i always have a feeling that you'll come back and that's what keeps me from moving on.

Seen just now

 0:10

I dont like it

You don't like anything

I like sleep and you

listen before you go

i read our old messages,
i laughed, then i cried.

Seen just now

every time my phone buzzes
i hope it's you missing me

listen before you go

every person has a breaking point,
mine was losing you..

Seen just now

because when i think of love, i only think
of it with you, maybe that's why i can't
think about it with anyone else

listen before you go

0:09

it's pathetic how much i still hope
it's you and me in the end

Seen just now

realizing you mean nothing to someone
after giving them your everything

— *how easy it is to be replaced*

listen before you go

i didn't mind waiting, if i knew
you were going to come back,
but i know you aren't...

Seen just now

▶ ⅰ||||ⅰ|||||·ⅰ·|·ⅰ|ⅰⅰⅰⅰⅰⅰ||ⅰⅰⅰ|·| 0:22

i'm moving on,
no more waiting,
no more hurt
if you wanted me,
you could've had me,
but you didn't
you blew your chance

listen before you go

just because we're not talking,
doesn't mean i don't miss you

Seen just now

wait until they break your heart.
wait to see how they justify it.
you'll see what kind of person
they are then.

listen before you go

0:06

i can feel you forgetting me..

Seen just now

 0:17

i wish i had the power to ignore you
like you ignore me

listen before you go

i still pretend that one day you'll wake up and you'll realize that i'm the one you want

Seen just now

▶ ·‧||||||‖|‖‧||‧||‧||‖|‖‖|‖|||‖ 0:08

she ignores you
but you like her.
she does nothing
yet you fall for her.
you miss her,
but she never
thought about you.

listen before you go

i forgive you, you will never forgive
yourself because i loved you and
you knew it.

Seen just now

▶ ⏺⏹⏺⏹⏺⏹⏺⏹⏺⏹⏺⏹⏺⏹⏺⏹ 0:28

and it was after
months of silence
that i realized
we make better
strangers than
we ever did
anything else

— *you're no good for me*

listen before you go

maybe when it's the right time
you will love me again

Seen just now

▶ ||||||||||||||||||••||||••|||||| 0:11

i want to go back
to a time before
you left

listen before you go

0:03

when i ignored you, i suffered more than you

Seen just now

i don't get it, you don't want me gone
but you don't want me with you either

listen before you go

when i first met you, i knew
that you'd either complete me
or completely destroy me.

Seen just now

▶ ·ᴵᴵᴵᴵᴵᴵᴵᴵᴵᴵᴵᴵᴵᴵᴵᴵᴵᴵᴵᴵᴵᴵᴵᴵᴵᴵ 0:17

when i first met you,
you were nothing more
than another face
but 6 months later
and you're the only face
i could ever find
in a crowded place

listen before you go

i hope, with every bone, in my body
that it'll be us, in the end

Seen just now

 0:22

so i guess it ends here,
we'll go our separate ways
and hope that we'll see each other
somewhere in the future

 0:11

i just want to talk.
i want to know what's going
through your head,
what you're thinking about.
i want to figure things out together.
just talking, no arguing, no fighting,
just talking like we used to,
i miss you.

Seen just now

i know my absence doesn't bother you
the way yours bothered me

I wish you knew how hard it was for me not to text you, when I want to talk to you so badly. Do you know how hard it is to stay busy enough so I dont think of you? Do you even know how hard it is for me not to tell you "I love you" even though I do? I love you more, than you deserve. I'm sorry if I care too much. I'm sorry for telling you about my pointless drama when you don't really care. Do you know how bad I wish you wanted me in your life the way I want you in mine?

Seen just now

0:22

i had so much left to say..

0:19

IM AM DONE WITH YOU. I'm done begging you to stay. I'm done waiting for you to come back be you ALWAYS make up an excuse. i'm done listening to your excuses because you ALWAYS find someone after that. IM DONE WITH YOUR LIES. Do not come into my life thinking it is okay to walk out thinking you didn't plan a future with me, thinking i didn't take those 3 words you told me EVERY night to heart. OFC I DID. DONT YOU DARE WALK OUT OF MY LIFE WITHOUT A MEANINGFUL APOLOGY. I am done wasting tears on you that don't need to be wasted. I'm done with your bs. I'm done having you in my life. I'm done with you controlling me, manipulating me, making me think the worst of myself. IM DONE. You lost me for good.

Seen just now

0:08

and our story has officially
ended, no going back

your chapter in my book is over, but
for some reason i can't flip the page

▶ ᴵᴵᴵᴵᴵᴵᴵᴵᴵᴵᴵᴵᴵᴵᴵᴵᴵᴵᴵᴵᴵᴵᴵᴵᴵᴵᴵ 0:28

even though you didn't make it to the end of
of my story, i will always have the corner
folded down on your page, because it was
one of my favorites

 0:22

dear Akhira, it's ironic as while in your company I had nothing to offer you other than my sarcasm and my constant banter, but now in your absence I have so many emotions in me I feel like I might burst from them,

im sorry for always putting an indifferent front, that was my way of hiding behind my feelings, you made me realise time means nothing, I felt more with you in the weeks we talked than with someone I spent years with,

thank you for always being there, for being you, for making me feel loved and looked after, for giving me your wisdom and more importantly your time, thank you for giving me a part of you that i swear to you I'll always cherish,

I'll remember every last second with you, the way you so gently treated me and how much you respected me, I'll remember the night you told me all about yourself while you laughed at me in that thick accented voice of yours when i'd tease you,

Seen just now

I'll remember your possessiveness and your protectiveness, I'll remember how I parted ways with being humble 2 days after we started talking, I'll remember your voice, your pain, your happiness, your writings— your writings that I'd spend sleepless nights reading but i never told you that, but I wish I did, I'll remember your potential and your talent, I'll remember you, for being you, and I'll answer two questions I always stubbornly left unanswered when we talked,

'Did you miss me?'
yes I did, I do, I always will, so very much
"what do you rate me?" infinity/10

thank you for being the dare demon that waltzed into my life, it was an honour akhu,

i hope you take care of yourself & find all the happiness and peace of both worlds, you'll always be in my prayers, & never give up what you're looking for because I believe in you, I always will, I hope you take care of yourself
— with love, your lil demon girl!

Seen just now

 0:38

i see you are writing about me even though you said nothing gets under your skin, it explains how you forced yourself into believing you're wasting my time so you'd find an excuse to cut communication,

i see the bits of our conversations in your writings even though you said you don't care, your name means the "afterlife" and I see it with how you express yourself,

"you're running through my head" you wrote

"at least I will know, you were thinking about me once" you wrote

akhira, I'll always remember you and everything you said to me, everything you entrusted me with, you weren't just a 4 am dare demon that waltzed into my life.

Seen just now

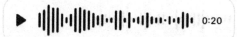 0:20

How are you?

How am I? How am I?? it's been a year,
365 days. I spent 365 days trying to
figure out what I did wrong. I spent 365
days trying to understand how you
could love me one day, and say you had
absolutely no feelings for me the next. I
spent this whole year trying to get over
you, thinking this year I would be okay,
and if I saw you, i wouldn't care.
But I'm still not over you. And I don't
think I ever will be. Because as much as
I try to deny it, you were and always will
be the love of my life...

Seen just now

listen before you go

just promise me one thing

what?

make sure he treats you better than i
did

Seen just now

 0:29

i still remember everything from the first time we met, from the voice recordings to the text messages. i don't regret meeting you but i regretted the way we always ended things. it pains me to see you leave because deep down i know i still love you, hoping that you'll be the one for me. i'm sorry i can't be the one you wanted and never will, i'm sorry for all the inconvenience i brought upon you. i find myself looking for you in someone else but none of them is just like you and honestly i'll wait but for how long more, i have no idea. i miss the way you made me smile, the way you made me feel so special and your assurance that you're always here for me, you made me the happiest i can be and i'll never forget you. i hope you're doing fine and like i promised, i'm always here if you ever need me.

Seen just now

 0:11

as my last act of love...

i accepted to leave so you could find the love
of your life, while i am letting mine go.

i can't escape the way i want you
words are not enough for "*i love you*"
so my tears replace the ink
making every page wet
but nothing will make you stay
even with the oceans i give
my brown eyes won't
turn blue for you
so i sink deeper
in memories
i can't forget
drowning in the absence
of what could have been
if you didn't leave me on read

▶ ·ıllıl|ıl|·l|l|ıl·|lı·ıl·|lı·ıl·|ıı· 0:17

i loved you but i was scared
so i never told you that
you blocked me on everything
but i would still pick up
if you called me back
since the 6th, you never did
and you never apologized
for making me feel used
you never apologized...
for anything you said
now i'm staying up to 3 am
wondering about the life
we could have had
bonded over poetry
and chocolate cake
what about june,
and the apartment
we were supposed to
move in to, now i'm
going through,
20.000 pictures
and i can't delete a single
one of them, working out till late pm's
throwing keys away, acting like i'm okay

▶ ⸰⫾⫿⫾⫾⫿⫾⫿⸱⫿⫿⫿⫾⫿⫿⫿⫿⫿⫿⫿⫿⫿⸱⫿⸱ 0:28

you cheated on me
i prayed it wasn't real...
you say he's the one
i wish you told me that
i hope he treats you better
than i ever did
but i can't sleep, knowing
you wake up next to him,
and i'm just
one bad day away
from breaking no contact
knowing you don't want me back
how much more pathetic
does it need to get
before i realize,
it's over, and
you are marrying him...

▶ ||l|ıı||||||ıı|ı|·|···ıı||·||···|ıı|ı|| 0:11

my eyes are heavy
from the tears
i can't shed
she took the light
with her when she left
now the darkness
can't be dimmed
pen emptied from ink
telling myself this is the last time
still i find myself begging god
for her to come back
please don't leave me
in the end
you and i,
prayed for the same things
i love you
for the rest of my life
remember
i'd still die
for you

▶ ⫾⫾⫾⫾⫾⫾⫾⫾⫾·⫾⫾⫾⫾⫾⫾⫾⫾⫾⫾⫾⫾⫾⫾⫾⫾⫾·⫾· 0:28

monday mornings
you used to train legs
i still remember everything
you said
even after deleting
every single text
i repeat it in my head
wishing you'd come back
but how can i pray for heaven
on earth, when i treated you bad
it's a love god won't save
and i can't accept, that
we not meant to be together again
so i listen to your voice message
hoping you'd say something else
you swore the last goodbye was the last
but memories sneaking out my eyes
won't let me forget
whatever we had,
can we just have it again?

▶ ⏸️|||·|||||||·||||·||·||·|||| 0:33

promised me you'd stay
but words don't mean much
when your absence is all there
is left to speak, and the silence
hurts more than anything
you could ever say to me
and i'm trying to remember
what happened that day
but broken piano's in my head
can't recreate the frequencies
of your voice, until i break every key,
there is no symphony left to play
but your words used to hold me
all the times you let me leave
wanted you to run after me
and i been staring at my phone
waiting for a text that won't come
laying in bed, regretting i deleted
every picture, i can't reforget how
you wrote about us,
already left, three times before,
wish you'd come back again
i don't wanna see you in the afterlife
i wanna see you right now, cause i found
paradise, in the garden of your eden eyes
prayers we shared, no one knows about
nights we stayed up, talked, and your
non stop laughter, made me happier

than anyone ever could, and i'm still holding on
to what you said, and what we promised
last september, i don't wanna say goodbye
cause i know this time you meant forever
blocking me from everywhere, we are less
than strangers, and i been screaming to god
begging for heaven on earth, cause i can't
let go, of that one glimpse of yours,
healed me more than any poem i wrote
you are still everything i want
and i will always wait for us to be together
because honestly i don't want anyone else
going through your birthday texts
and i can't find peace in
deleting it or forgetting
what you said
told me to never reach out again
but i can't stay away from you
even if hell is put between us
i would run, with no cold feet,
or hesitation at all...
and i can't find closure
in the last voice message
you sent a week ago
so i cry and call you again
even with no dial tone
till your friends tells me
to leave you alone
...
and i swore i would
but i already promised god
i would never give up on us

▶ ||||•||||||||•||•||•••||||••||||•|| 0:11

and in art
i find a glimmer of hope
in a place we can still exist
my prayers for you won't end
even if we not meant to be
i will defy destiny
so it becomes
a + z

▶ ||||||||||||||||||||·||···||||||| 0:11

maybe one day
you will find
the memories
in the back of your mind
and reach out like the old times
while wet glimpses slip out my eyes,
looking at her, i still see your smile
you were beyond the painting
out the frames of art,
couldn't contain it, in poems
so my tears races to the paper
to express what words won't
when poetry is not enough
for you to stay, so i leave
the last page blank
in case, you come back

— 06.02.2024

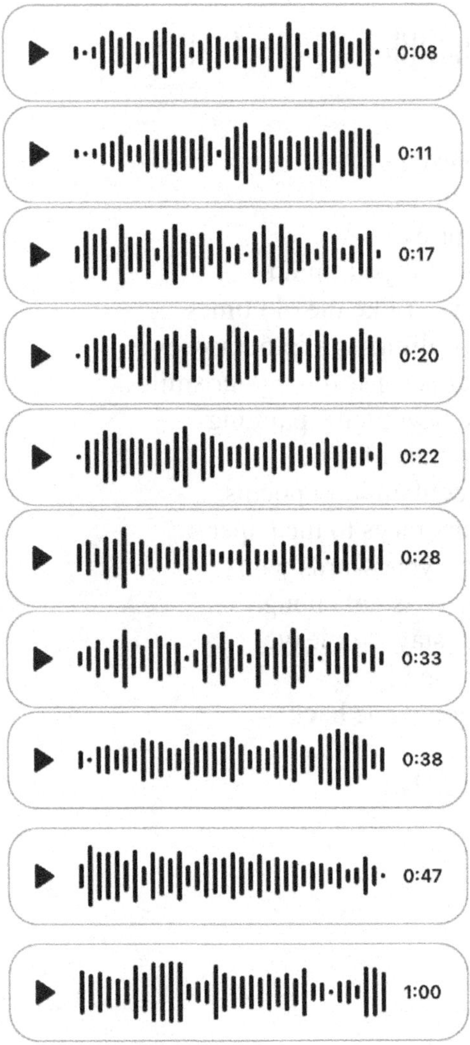
0:08
0:11
0:17
0:20
0:22
0:28
0:33
0:38
0:47
1:00

akhira

Made in the USA
Monee, IL
31 July 2024

63059389R00116